Love Poem to Tofu
    & Other Poems

Love Poem to Tofu

& Other Poems

Mộng-Lan

Copyright © 2007 by Mong-Lan
All rights reserved. No part of this book may be used or reproduced without the permission of the author.

ISBN: 978-0-6151-4656-0

Second Edition
Printed in the United States of America

Calligraphic art by Mong-Lan
www.monglan.com

Cover, book design, and author photo: Mong-Lan

Published by
Valiant Press
P.O. Box 2771
Sugar Land, Texas 77487

For lovers of food, my family, and J.A.

Contents

Love Poems

Love Poem to Tofu 3
Love Poem to Red Chili Peppers 4
Love Poem to *Bun Rieu* 5
Love Poem to Spinach 7
Love Poem to *Banh Cuon* 8
Love Poem to Thick Rice Noodles 10
Love Poem to Shitake 11
Love Poem to Broccoli 13
Love Poem to *Café au Lait* 14
Love poem to Green Tea 16

One Thousand Minds Brimming

Proof 19
A Bamboo Knife 21
Bangkok: City Streets 24
Bangkok: Royalty 27
Bangkok: River 29
Bangkok [neon lights] 31
Sentient Figure 33
Mountain Mysticism 35
Leblon-Ipanema-Copacabana: Rio de Janeiro 38

Notes 42

Acknowledgements

Grateful acknowledgements to the editors of the following journals and literary magazines where my poems first appeared:

The Antioch Review, "Bangkok [neon lights]."
Artful Dodge, "love poem to thick rice noodles."
Cimarron Review, "Love Poem to Shitake Mushroom"; "Love Poem to Broccoli"; "Love Poem to Green Tea."
Colorado Review, "Love Poem to Spinach."
Constellation, "Leblon-Ipanema-Copacabana"; "Mountain Mysticism."
Da Mau, www.damau.org, "Love Poem to *Banh Cuon*"; "Love Poem to *Bun Rieu*."
Kenyon Review, "Bangkok: City Streets"; "Bangkok: Royalty."
Nha Magazine, "Love Poem to Café au Lait";"Love Poem to Red Chili Peppers."
Nhip Song, "A Bamboo Stick;" "Love Poem to Tofu."
Seneca Review, "Proof."

I would like to thank my parents, especially my mother, for all the stories of our family, those of my great grandparents to those of my grandparents, and for teaching me the rudiments of Vietnamese cooking. I would like to thank J.A., for being there to enjoy all our adventurous meals together and for everything else. Many thanks to you, my friends, for your kind and gracious support.

Love Poems

Love Poem to Tofu

       everyday i open you up
          with a knife slice you in half boil eat you

O how i need you warm creamy-white loaded with vegetable protein
           how can i live
   without your textured taste?
      i don't even remember
           when we first met: it must've been
    in Saigon in a soup dish my mother made with tomatoes
          & a solitary
               flaming egg
    for many years i knew you made in California not as
    good as in Vietnam but now in Tokyo you once again
    become divine

  you are exquisite plain dipped in soy sauce or *nuoc mam*
              with a bit of lemon
      & cayenne pepper

varieties of you i love silken firm braised

              tofu i feast upon you

Love Poem to Red Chili Peppers

your red hot tongue
slips into my mouth   sometimes
                unknowingly   you explode with each bite
all your diversions & fireworks   your petulant sting

i can't adequately extol you
for you are a paradox   your unassuming tongue brings terror
to most people but to me brings
       ecstasy.
                            where did you receive all your
                powers?
perhaps from the ubiquitous Sun
                you pack in her rays

i am in love with your arias   penetrating deeply
        clearing me up for other pleasures

Love Poem to *Bun Rieu*

        a bowl of *bun rieu*   eaten at *Cho Lon*

    rice vermicelli in a rich broth of tomatoes shrimp & crabmeat

                          eating my way into memory a moth
              i remember
every delicious sliver of rice vermicelli
              every succulent morsel
              every slurp

                              my lost city
                  under broth and soup

      cousins dying at sea or far away
                          escaping one's country

        loss is all-encompassing
                down to the last drop

Love Poem to Spinach

                                        your vulgar name is "Spinach" but your
               glorious Latinate name is *Spinacia Oleracea*
                                                 of the goosefoot family

your large   dark-green juicy   edible leaves are beacons
                                        sending tremors through my body

am i masochistic? loving you that most hate—

                i took to liking you immediately
                              then the love came later   stronger

       i find you absolutely necessary: your stalks & leaves full of iron

      you are luscious
                      sweet
          divine
                                    you empower anyone
                                            who eats you

     close to your original glory
                              is how i want you

Love Poem to *Banh Cuon*

        i learned to make you once & you were difficult
                        nothing worth it is easy

    when i was young   in Saigon & in little Saigons in America
        i ate you with minced pork
                mushrooms   prawn

you are delicate   white layers of flimsy rice film   like white wings
                            ready to fly
              wherever the eater wishes

    a special treat   we devoured you on Sunday
mornings as if there was nothing
        left on earth

they were the days in which there was nothing to do no yearning
        but being with family
                nothing to wish for but luxuriating
      in the fish sauce
      spiked with chili peppers and lemons
                    the days of youth

now   when find you   i eat you vegetarian style   without meat
        with a concoction of soy sauce lemon & chili peppers

    i linger over your melting body
      in my mouth
             take your labia   &
                    swallow

Love Poem to Thick Rice Noodles

O your thick body luscious as a pillow
        in base of tomato & shrimp
                my tongue glides over your cellophane

      under large blue umbrellas
          in Saigon i eat you
with crabmeat soft & chewy   while the youths with AK guns strapped
              over their shoulders motorcycles thundering on

      in East Palo Alto   i eat you
          in a sautéed dish with garlic onions tofu & leek

              while hearing gun shots
                  police sires   ambulances
plangent trucks passing in front of my house

Love Poem to Shitake

who are you, really?
    you are so elusive   like Pluto the moon

lunar disked
        you were there
ready to greet me early
      in the world

        my first experience
  of you   though from desiccated form
were filling enough
     but in Japan   i discovered you
      fresh
as the day is plump   juicy
         & whole
    fighting cancer   building bones
cleaning blood you make me stronger
   than i would be

    luscious
  fungus you are sweet
       unapologetic

secretly growing in the enigmatic dark

       is where you get your power
     exuding confidence
in fried rice soups stir fries spring rolls

        in everything i surrender

       to you my utmost care
                     preparing you for the meal

              to you   i surrender
    your delicate umber
                           stout umbrellas
            thick protective legs

                   yes you are physically obtuse
but love is in the mouth
       not in the eyes

Love Poem to Broccoli

        insensate   you are   bringing me over
                                              like this

your dominant curlicues
                        are green   placid
              your crunch soothing to the spine

      cancer-fighting
your scintillating frilly-green dresses
              little heads blooming   undress before me

            how delicious you are
                            how full of potassium!

  spirited
       you are erect   muscular
                bunchy with blossoms   little promises waiting
              to be fulfilled

Love Poem to *Café au Lait*

you wake me up every morning
        with your creaminess & smooth
                talking body   brown
  & supple   muscles
              dexterous   inviting
                      your caramel & froth
    sing to me in French
        and i sing in French all day Edith Piaf
    her sparrowlike songs
            with a bit of sugar   it is amazing
        how you bring me to an addictive frenzy

white frizzy fuzz   your brown-white
            moustache   your milky otherness
    your stunning inkiness
        that would write odes   ballads   and novels
    that would build railroads
& skyscrapers   fences & automobiles   skyrockets
                      Civilization itself

you are nothing like the *café sua*
        of my Saigon   which is exceedingly sweet
bitter   & concentrated   like Saigon itself

O *Café au Lait*   i know you hum
        sweet nothings and ideas
    into other's ears
             i only wait for you to drive
    me crazy   inflict an ulcer
        perhaps i should give you up
            for something more gentle   faithful
    like green tea?

Love poem to Green Tea

                                      smooth   unassuming   low-key

i have left *café au lait* for you darling

                   left the coffee bean for your complicated
yet pure leaf

          your body   emerald   tranquil   a slant rhyme

underneath this clear verdigris   is your inner self

             underneath the unassuming demeanor is your prudent
                  uniqueness   your discreet fluid whispers

        you give me strength in the mornings
                when the day is low   you give me energy

your powers so steady they are enacted without the drinker's knowing

          sleek   lustrous   sage   sending me waves of bright
                           undulating consciousness

One Thousand Minds Brimming

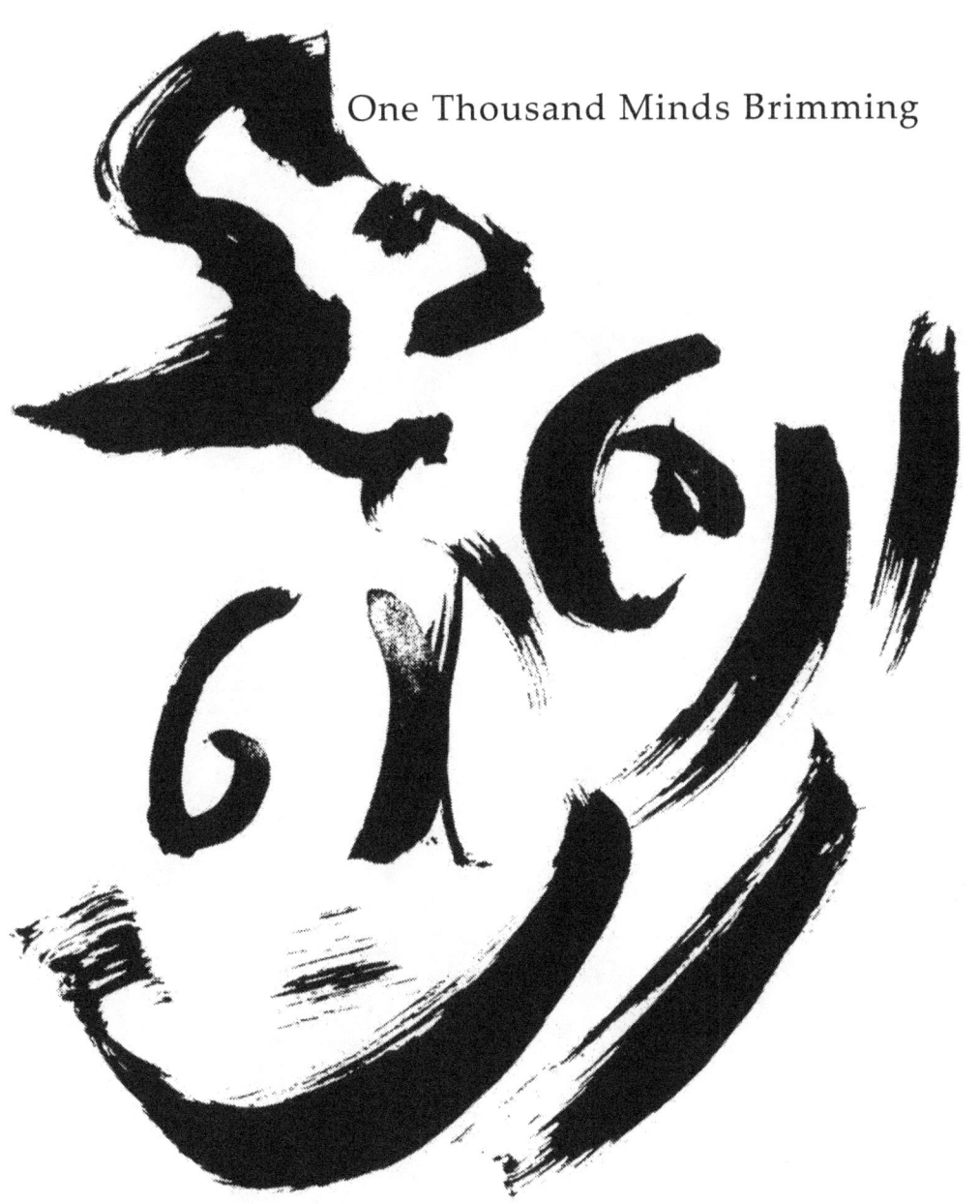

Proof

                                            in this city where you do not live
                  you were born
                              the city itself no longer exists on a map
                      of Vietnam
the street on which you were
              born does not exist
                                for its name has changed
                  if you had continued
        to exist here if you had stayed after war's end
now 30 yrs later you would be walking down the street talking
                          joking philosophizing suffering with friends
           you would be a closed-eyed bicycle-motor-riding adult
               married with children

                      the house where you lived   the first five years
             of your life was seized
                     & therefore does not exist
             as you knew it
it sits on a street whose name has changed
          no longer recognizable

                                your grandparent's house
         also appropriated
   now people exist there eating making love defecating
              spinning new lives for themselves from the walls
     of your past

     in the city where you were born
            you do not now exist because the city
                          no longer exists

          the grandparents whom you met

                              in your imagination

         & memory did exist
                              & gave birth to your parents
who exist in a different country & plane altogether
         not in this city

                    of faint turquoise   limestone   whiteness &   charcoal
                                        of your imagination

                                             two handfuls of cities
                    changed names through wars or revolutions

the hospital where you were born still remains
                              that exists & still keeps
               its name   Hospital of Saint Paul

                              does that prove anything?

A Bamboo Knife

    to cut the umbilical cord
            but what to cut the hysteria   the mania the melancholia?

Great Grandmother Le Thi Hai born December 7, 1878
        died June 17, 1962.
Ha Dong North Vietnam

A spoon to carve out the child   from rice & malaria
    a bag of bones to sink the body down
a scythe to kill someone with
        a map of the moon to go thereafter

§

        From each birth   bloodletting

each baby alive to this world
      for a few days   and then returned to the ether
            world   without names or
            bodies

      Only one survived

           Five fetuses   five years
    of being bloated   five years
      of carrying

       The midwife cut each umbilical cord with bamboo
                                          each time

           The baby turned porcelain blue stopped breathing
                               after a few days
                  infection   tetanus

                  Only one was strong enough to survive
                          infancy

  My body
        could not take the grief
               Trembling crying I buried each dead
                    child in the cemetery
                            I was loud   brash   given to fits
                  & sadness

§

1954

My only child his wife my grandchildren   they have all
        left

    They have all gone
                not given me word

While sleeping I dreamt of emptiness a void an empty egg a coffin
      then when I woke up
                they were all gone

        My child left me   the only one
                                bold enough to survive

Do they blame me for having a tongue?
                            Perhaps they wanted to cut
    my tongue   cut my voice

                            Where have they gone?

                I pull out my hair I scream
                            for the ancestors anybody
                      to hear

§

Then the soldiers came they seized my house
                took my land   took all my possessions
                          consigned me to tree behind my house
                                        made me eat dirt

Thank Buddha
    I was so old   the soldiers left my shriveled sex alone

                they chewed
                        my tongue and spat it out

Bangkok: City Streets

The silk maker walked
    into the forest & never returned

       §

   Making love to you   natural clean

       Did you think to bring happiness?

Morning's burgeoning mass—
   how rare it is to see the light of a thousand minds brimming

       Mad *tuk tuks* roaring swerving
  wildly in pitch to long tailed boats on
     Chao Phraya River River of Kings

Emaciated cats
  babies all of them elusively slink

     Elephants walk
       pavements
  begging
      for sugarcane &
        the men riding them

§

Walk on *Charoen Krung* Road

Machinery of noise as if in a vault   cars running
up your nervous system   up your veins   echo of
        grime echo of industry clamoring up buildings   noises metallic
                & clanking rubbing against each other

                        In the vortex young men walk
                proud   erect   youthful

Bangkok: Royalty

O incongruous city! Bangkok roars
                                          with a bang!

    Disco Elephants—O king of the forest

You walk with feet pounding
        city cement   the world's weight on you   beggars
                              the destitute

§

Ogling taxi drivers   loud-mouthed gap-toothed buildings
                              3 scrawny dogs sleeping in street crevices
a dog on corner   sleeping on noise & depravity

        3 lonely dogs on the streets   crooning their loves

                Boats tug a V in the water

        a Chinese spy angles in for a joke

§

                          A taxi driver with bad energy   drunk
            behind the wheel   O bustling river

                                           & the glass eyed King

peering unfathomable from colossal framed portraits
                     next to his queen
             at the swarm of people

Bangkok: River

                      "the bandits' muzzle flash singed
                              your jet black hair"

Christmas Eve   lepered people
      sit on Bangkok boulevards with nubs for hands
                                eyes smeared into flesh
                          barely with feet
             begging

Multifarious colored lights   cheesy yuletide ornaments
      overflow the streets

Girls & women abound   beautiful   girls   women
                          selling themselves cheap

                §

From his traditional Thai house of old teak   the American silk maker
      walked into the forest & did not return

                §

O city of forever   stretching beyond your years

O river of commerce   *Chao Phraya*   of ten thousand barges   nosing
                              down the river aquiline fashion

Meditating on this river   more than a thousand years old

        long tailed boats in splendorous bright reds blues oranges
   & sky trains criss-crossing the heavens

                Pyramids of gold rise from the shores
      of the river's stirrings

Bangkok [neon lights]

O the orchids of Bangkok!

      O the luxuriant ladyboys   their devilish seductive smiles

            O the decadence   the freedoms of Bangkok!
                  your serpentine ways

into another unawares our embrace defined night-days

                  one thinks in embraces
young girls from the village pretend to be go-go girls

                      naked from waist up

              city girls completely naked
Go-go girls dancing like embarrassed sardines

in the lady-boy club   an effervescent pretend land   Miss Brazil
    Miss Mexico   Miss France   Miss Singapore
       surgically amplified

in another bar
        birds breathless up cunts
            ping pong balls inserted   being thrown out

                    birds flying out of cunts

    needles & needles being pulled out of cunts

                          a whole string of sharp needles

            razors being pulled out   a whole string
                                          of razors being pulled out

Sentient Figure

Wood Sculpture, Standing figure, 14-17th century, Indonesia

Ironwood man   boogie man

    standing hands behind your ears   mouth gaping

        Listen Man!

                Hear the ants
                    you know them intimately
                Tribal enemies skinning on
                      the other coast

Knower   Listener

        To what do you listen

        What do you hear?

        How are we destroying ourselves
            tell me this

      The world's forests recede into a baldness

                Waves recede with great
        momentum

There is no way into the other world but by listening   watching

                nothing to do but
                    BREATHE

Breathe   listen to the forest leaves rustling

Breathe   listen to the iron lungs of the world   wooden lungs
                of the forests
                                        red muscular lungs of roots

            beating hearts of skittish cats
                                loyal hearts of buffalo wading
                        the whoosh of unrelenting waves

        Families have gone   evacuated

Fierce winds   blow   howling man

                                        Quiet Man!

A great man-eating wave has come!

Mountain Mysticism

1

    shuffling suede footprints
                      snarled coyote's tongues

mountain's clustered knuckles
        blanket a land shooting haikus

              rubber shoes leave behind thoughts   fishhook of
                                      dust blown questing

a lady notes the spectacular view
                      slashed granite & lichen curdling

the "phoneline trail"
        grinds muscles
                down moving slopes upwardly sloping

            desert flowers red velvet against dirt

a yellow breeze fosters green lichen

                          death like sweat
    over the saguaro's proud & lusty stubble
        burnt out thick saguaro man with too many arms

2

    you have scaled to the top   rocks carved by rain

range by heat & plodding feet of strangers

    so many have trod here over rim stubble created by
                                    exhaustion &   avalanches

       wind warp tethers dirt in eyes

                                              scares ghostly feet

words crusted from lips straggling on dust paths

ancient eyes carved this path through the Sabino canyons albino & wise

       a rock kicked out of place   pocketed as souvenir

3

     stone
             matter haunted with sounds
                             voice-eating

           shuffling eyes howling like coyotes

4

if we are not all travelers what are we?

                      if we are not ultimately ephemeral   what are we?

if not travelers from another world   which world?

                                  we are permanence itself

Tucson, Arizona, 2000

Leblon-Ipanema-Copacabana: Rio de Janeiro

Blessed sand form of glass speckling clothes
                            insensate particle of time You skirt
over the earth flitting keenfully

O-cean insatiate being your salt waters divulge in our veins creatures
      from the depths

The energy field around your lofty-peaked
       mountains accumulate over time receiving sun's rays
         still

              Trees miraculous lush—beacon of greenlight
      Purespirit cathedral
            of sounds   august ethereal mindstrings

Eyelashes lips earth mountains of breasts   valleys of buttocks
              magnificent g-strings entrusting all to look

              Sun   lifegiver   entreat us to love
                  the earth as we all should

§

      Rio the river a name for a city mistakenly named   is tender
                        as a lover in the mornings

How to find the names of places visited never revisited?

How to shovel away at our lives to find the smallest particle
      representative of the whole what is dearest?

Backs to sand we listen to dreams & nightmares

The smells of ocean sand &
                sex on the beach

                                  samba heart beating Bodies
                      pulsating gyrating
                          Such delirium such happiness
      Cariocas cavort in preparation for Carnaval
Samba music carries hips & buttocks at nanoseconds *Cariocas* feasting
                    on lyrics & sweaty skin one another's
touch beat within the beat   musicians bleating throbbing
      blowing strumming

§

So many colors under the sun so many suns: Portuguese moonskin
         potatochipskin mulatto skin dark skin & the world
                      sees itself a mosaic of flaming rain
     Garota de Ipanema a cheap joint where artists sit & drink
       to death
            next to hills that jut into air
                   of mist & men & women running

§

Not of this earth   luminous yet living
closest to the gods to God crosses borders walking on water

                         A life led in many places
                              simultaneously

Notes

Page 5, *Bun Rieu* is crabmeat noodle soup, from northern Vietnam.

Page 8, *Banh cuon* (rice flour steamed rolls) is a northern Vietnamese dish, hailing from Thanh Tri district just outside Hanoi. Minced pork, mushrooms and prawns are wrapped in a flimsy rice film. It comes served with sliced cucumber, *cha lua*, beansprouts, sprinkled with deep-fried shallots and chopped mint with a *nuoc mam* (fish sauce) dip.

Page 33, "Sentient Figure" was commissioned by the Dallas Museum of Art, based on a sculpture of the same name in its permanent collection. In 2005, I was the Museum's inaugural Poet and Visual Artist in Residence. For six months, my paintings and photographs were exhibited in the Museum in a show entitled, "The World of Mong-Lan."

About the Author

Born in Vietnam, poet, writer, painter, photographer, and Argentine tango dancer, Mong-Lan left her native country on the last day of the evacuation of Saigon in 1975. Author of *Song of the Cicadas* (winner of the 2000 Juniper Prize, the 2002 Great Lakes Colleges Association's New Writers Awards for Poetry, and a finalist for the Poetry Society of America's Norma Farber Award), *Why is the Edge Always Windy?* and *Tango: a Seismology* (forthcoming), she received her Master of Fine Arts from the University of Arizona, was the recipient of a Wallace E. Stegner Fellowship in poetry for two years at Stanford University, and was a Fulbright Grantee in Vietnam. Her poetry has been anthologized in *Best American Poetry; The Pushcart Book of Poetry: Best Poems from 30 Years of the Pushcart Prize; Asian American Poetry: the Next Generation; Contemporary Voices from the Eastern World: an Anthology of Poems*, and has appeared in leading American literary journals. Her paintings and photographs have been exhibited for one year in the Capitol House in Washington D.C., in galleries in the San Francisco Bay Area, the Museum of Fine Arts in Houston, for six months at the Dallas Museum of Art, and in public exhibitions in Tokyo, Bali, and Seoul. Mong-Lan has taught at the University of Arizona, Stanford University, and the University of Maryland in Tokyo. She also has given scores of readings and academic presentations in the United States, Japan, Korea, Indonesia, Malaysia, Germany, Switzerland, and Argentina.

Visit: www.monglan.com

www.ingramcontent.com/pod-product-compliance
Lightning Source LLC
Chambersburg PA
CBHW020023050426
42450CB00005B/616